I0406965

The Mindful Leader
Inspiring Mental Wellness in the Workplace

Table of Contents

Chapter 1. Introduction

In an increasingly demanding workplace environment, one element consistently stands out as a determining factor for success: mental wellness. This Special Report, titled "The Mindful Leader: Inspiring Mental Wellness in the Workplace," aims to shed a new light on this vital subject. Not only does it delve into the rapidly evolving understanding of mental health, but it also showcases how leaders can inspire their teams to embrace a positive state of mind. By turning workplace stress into an opportunity for growth and productivity, companies can thrive in unprecedented ways. Encapsulating insightful studies, cutting-edge techniques, practical tips, and inspiring stories of transformation, this report provides a road map for all who aspire to lead their organizations with empathy and inspiration. Discover how to harness the power of a mindful leadership approach, encourage mental wellness, and foster a uniquely positive company culture. Through a simple change in perspective, enhance your leadership style, and turn your workplace into an environment of creativity, innovation, and well-being. Your journey towards becoming a mindful leader begins here. Choose well-being, choose success. This report, full of potential, can be your compass to navigate this exhilarating journey. Get your copy today!

Chapter 2. Introduction to Mindful Leadership

In this dynamically evolving workspace, the concept of Mindful Leadership emerges as a beacon of change, empathy, and psychological wellness. It's incumbent upon us as progressive individuals to delve into this revolutionary leadership style and comprehend its significance for the organizations today and the teams they are entrusted with.

2.1. Fundamentals of Mindful Leadership

Mindful leadership is about cultivating attention to the present, fostering an attitude that is non-judgmental, patient, and curious. It's rooted in the practice of mindfulness which is about being fully aware of the present moment, enabling leaders to take mindful action instead of reacting impulsively or on auto-pilot.

Building personal mindfulness skills as a leader, such as focused attention, compassion, and emotional regulation, not only enhances personal resilience but also allows you to create an environment that encourages creativity, innovation, and the ability to thrive during challenging times.

2.2. The Rising Need for Mindful Leadership

The modern workplace can be a source of innovative ideas and creativity, but also stress and burnout. With a rapidly changing environment, individuals find themselves struggling to adapt and maintain balance. This is where mindful leadership can play a significant role - teaching individuals to manage their internal state amidst the external chaos.

Cases of stress, anxiety, and other mental health issues are on the rise, signaling the need for reactive measures in professional spaces. The need for leaders who are sensitive to this surge in mental health issues and are adept at providing guidance and support is also growing. Consequently, leadership that emphasizes empathy, compassion, and mental well-being is no longer just a positive addition; it is a necessity.

2.3. Mindful Leadership and Performance

The application of mindfulness in leadership can render exceptional results in terms of performance and productivity. As human beings, our tendency to multitask to meet the demands of a fast-paced world often leads to a scattered mind and reduced efficiency. However, by focusing on the present moment, we can give our complete attention to one task, enhancing the quality of work.

By cultivating mindfulness, leaders can help improve concentration, understand their team better, and provide realistic and achievable goals. Results drawn from various studies indicate that practicing mindfulness can improve cognitive abilities, response time, and decision-making skills, subsequently contributing to higher productivity and overall performance.

2.4. Role of Emotional Intelligence in Mindful Leadership

Emotional intelligence plays a crucial role in the development of mindful leadership. Leaders who have high emotional intelligence are better equipped to manage their own emotions and understand the emotions of their team members. They have the capacity to acknowledge and respect diversity in thoughts, feelings, and expression, thus contributing to a vibrant and motivated work environment.

Emotional intelligence goes hand in hand with mindfulness as both require an acute sense of awareness of one's surroundings as well as introspective understanding. Such self-awareness leads to more controlled reactions, better interpersonal communication, and empathy – all of which are important tenets of effective leadership.

2.5. The Pillars of Mindful Leadership

There are primarily three key pillars of mindful leadership - Attention, Intention, and Attitude. Attention refers to where we decide to direct our focus. For a mindful leader, it implies keeping the mind in the present moment, effectively focusing on the task at hand while consciously acknowledging and quickly letting go of interruptions.

Intention refers to the mental state that influences our actions. It is about being aware of our underlying motivations and consciously choosing ones that are beneficial or positive. Mindful leaders set clear, ethical, and inclusive intentions that can positively shape their decisions and actions.

The third pillar, Attitude, encapsulates our worldview. A mindful leader maintains an attitude of innate curiosity, patience, compassion, and non-judgement towards themselves and others. Such an attitude lets them remain open-minded, quickly adapt to change, and foster a team culture that encourages growth and innovation.

2.6. Leading by Example

A mindful leader always leads by example - setting a personal precedent for behavior, work ethic, and values. When leaders embrace mindfulness, they reduce their own stress levels, increase their emotional intelligence and improve their decision-making ability. This directly impacts the team they lead, promoting a work culture that acknowledges the importance of mental health and individual well-being.

By discussing their own journeys toward mindfulness, leaders can inspire their teams to adopt these practices. This may include sharing personal experiences with stress and how mindfulness helped, or discussing books and resources that have aided their personal growth.

In conclusion, mindful leadership is all about leading with awareness, compassion, and focus. This results in not only enhancing the leaders' resilience, emotional intelligence, and decision-making abilities but also fosters a positive, stress-free, and supportive work environment that values employee well-being. This understanding, therefore, warrants a closer look at how we can master the art of mindful leadership, which we will examine in the forthcoming chapters.

Chapter 3. The Brain Science Behind Mindfulness

To delve into a comprehensive understanding of mindfulness, it's critical to approach it through the lens of neuroscience. What might seem to be a straightforward practice of concentrated attention turns out to be a complex dance of neural processes, all coming together to shape the brain and behavior. These are not just abstract concepts; the science of mindfulness has direct implications on how leaders can create supportive workplaces that enhance employee mental wellness.

3.1. The Neuroscience of Mindfulness

Mindfulness is the act of consciously focusing your mind on the present moment without judgment or reaction. This act of centering oneself cultivates awareness to the entire range of experience, including sensations, thoughts and feelings, and the surrounding environment.

Based on neuroscientific studies, mindfulness has the potential to significantly alter the structure and function of the brain, bolstering qualities such as focus, emotional intelligence, and stress resilience. Scientists have identified several key brain regions that are modified through regular mindfulness practice.

3.2. Prefrontal Cortex and Attention Regulation

The prefrontal cortex (PFC) is involved in executive functions such as planning, decision making, and regulating attention. Typically, it works in tandem with other brain regions to regulate emotions and maintain focus. Research has shown that mindfulness practice can bolster the functioning of the PFC.

A 2007 study published in Neuroreport found that long-term mindfulness practitioners have thicker prefrontal cortices compared to non-practitioners. This implies the enhanced cognitive capacities such as attentiveness and decision making associated with this brain region.

3.3. The Amygdala and Emotional Regulation

The amygdala, almond-shaped clusters of interconnected structures in the deeper parts of the brain, is crucial for emotional processing. Stressful experiences can stimulate the amygdala, inducing anxiety, fear, or anger responses.

With mindfulness, the emotional reactions from these stimuli can be regulated. Studies suggest that mindfulness decreases amygdala reactivity to emotional triggers and aids in better management of stress responses.

Moreover, a 2011 study published in Psychiatry Research shows that individuals who underwent mindfulness-based stress reduction training had reduced amygdala volumes compared to those who didn't participate in the training. This indicates how mindfulness can help attenuate emotional responses and cultivate emotional stability.

3.4. The Hippocampus and Memory Processing

The hippocampus plays a vital role in memory processing and is particularly sensitive to stress. Chronic stress can result in the shrinkage of the hippocampus, leading to memory problems and increased risk for certain mental disorders like depression and post-traumatic stress disorder.

Mindfulness practices lead to an increase in hippocampal density, according to a study published in Psychiatry Research: Neuroimaging. By combating the negative effects of stress on the hippocampus, mindfulness can improve memory functions and emotional regulation.

3.5. The Default Mode Network and Self-Referential Thinking

Our brains have a default mode network (DMN), activated when we engage in self-referential thinking (thinking about self) or when the mind is left to wander. Excessive activity in the DMN can lead to rumination and worry.

A study in the Proceedings of the National Academy of Sciences found that mindfulness practice reduces activity in DMN, bringing about a more focused and less self-centric perspective. This shift is extremely helpful in reducing stress levels, depression, and enhancing overall cognitive function.

3.6. Mindfulness, Neuroplasticity, and Change

Beyond impacting individual brain regions, mindfulness promotes neuroplasticity – the brain's ability to reorganize itself by forming new neural connections. Mindfulness effectively strengthens the resilience of the brain, making it more adaptable to stress and adversity.

A study in the Journal of Neurophysiology found that mindfulness practitioners had enhanced neuroplasticity, which directly correlated with improved attention, cognitive flexibility, and mental well-being.

In summary, the brain science behind mindfulness reveals how this practice isn't just a psychological tool—it's a catalyst for enhancing brain health and function. Given the right understanding and implementation, mindfulness can be a pathway to foster mental wellness in the workplace, molding leaders who are not only mindful but also psychologically resilient and empathic. This lays the foundation for a positive workplace environment, where employees feel supported, motivated, and engaged.

Chapter 4. Understanding Mental Wellness in the Workplace

In any organization, it's essential to understand the concept of mental wellness. Mental wellness refers to your mental state, how you are feeling emotionally and how well you can function in your day-to-day life. As part of being mindful leaders, understanding this concept is an imperative step. This is the first stepping stone to carving a better future for your workforce that enables growth and productivity while fostering empathy.

4.1. Understanding Mental Wellness

An often overlooked aspect, mental wellness is as critical for productivity and organizational success as physical health. It's not just about the absence of mental health disorders. It refers to the presence of positive characteristics, such as the ability to manage stress, the capability to learn new things, the strength to bounce back from adversity, the capacity to build and maintain relationships, and the power to achieve one's goals.

Mental wellness encompasses various dimensions, each of which contributes to an individual's overall well-being. It ranges from the mental, emotional, and social well-being. In essence, it's all about how individuals think, feel, and behave. Wellness or the lack of it can significantly influence how employees handle stress, relate to others, and make choices. Mental wellness is crucial at every phase of life, from adolescence through adulthood, and is deeply connected to work life because a significant portion of adult life is spent in the workspace.

4.2. Importance of Mental Wellness

Attending to mental wellness in the workplace is no longer a luxury; instead, it is a necessity. The modern workplace is fraught with challenges that can lead to stress, burnout, and eventually to more severe psychological conditions such as depression, anxiety, and even suicide.

Studies have shown that organizations that attend to the psychological well-being of their employees have higher rates of productivity, reduce absenteeism, and improve job satisfaction. Enhanced mental wellness leads to an increase in collaboration, creativity, adaptability—all traits that are invaluable for organizations that intend to better cope with the increasing pace of change and unpredictability in the business environment.

Mental wellness is an essential element in sustaining employees' job performance. It also plays a significant role in fostering a positive work environment, which eventually reflects on the quality of work, productivity, and the overall success of the organization.

4.3. Mental Wellness Challenges in Contemporary Workplaces

Workplace-related stress is one of the most significant challenges facing employees today. Accentuated by globalization, technology, and the 24/7 work environment, workplace stress has taken a toll on employees' mental wellness across the globe.

The evolving work environment contributes towards increasing expectations, job insecurity, long working hours, lack of work-life balance and interpersonal conflicts — all of these accumulates into a distressing work environment, leading to increased stress and burnout.

Mental health disorders resulting from stress are on the rise and have significant repercussions for individuals and organizations. These disorders can lead to decreased productivity due to absenteeism, presenteeism (being physically present at work but not fully engaged or productive), and increased health-related costs.

4.4. Strategies to Enhance Mental Wellness

Embracing a culture of mental wellness requires a multi-pronged approach. It involves creating a supportive workplace environment, providing resources for mental wellness, facilitating work-life balance, promoting open conversations about mental wellness, and proactively addressing issues related to workplace stress.

Companies can invest in training programs that enhance employees' resilience and stress management skills. Organizations could also provide services like counselling to help employees manage personal or professional challenges that impact their mental wellness.

Promoting a culture of respect, inclusivity, and diversity can significantly foster mental wellness. Ensuring a supportive work environment where every employee is respected for their individuality and contribution can reduce incidents of workplace tension and conflict.

Furthermore, facilitating a good work-life balance is critical. Companies need to ensure that employees have ample opportunities to decompress and balance their job responsibilities with their personal lives. This might include permitting flexible work hours, enabling remote work options or just ensuring that there is no expectation to engage in work-related tasks outside of normal work hours.

Mental wellness has far-reaching impacts that extend beyond

productivity and workplace satisfaction. It affects each individual personally and contributes to interpersonal relationships within the workplace.

Taking the initiative to prioritize mental wellness demonstrates an organization's commitment towards its employees' health and well-being. Indeed, with an insightful understanding of mental wellness, organizations can harness the benefits of a happier, healthier, and more productive workforce. In doing so, they're just not creating a revitalizing environment to work in but developing leaders who are mentally fit to guide their teams towards progress.

Chapter 5. The Role of Leadership in Cultivating Mental Well-being

Intermingling the concepts of leadership and mental well-being may seem unconventional, even revolutionary, but it is precisely in this fusion that a unique opportunity for growth emerges. Leaders, who are often considered the source of direction, can also be the catalysts for a mental wellness-oriented culture shift.

5.1. The Intersection of Leadership and Mental Well-being

Historically, leadership has been associated with power, authority, and decision-making. In contrast, mental well-being has often been relegated to the confines of personal life and neglected in professional settings. However, as the modern workplace evolves, so does the understanding of these two ideas and their interplay.

Creating a mentally healthy workplace requires intentional effort, and leadership is in the unique position of shaping that effort's direction and impact. More than ever, leaders are being called upon to implement strategies that promote the mental well-being of their teams. The need for such strategies arises from two major shifts.

Firstly, the contemporary workplace landscape is marked by rapid change, technological advancement, and an ever-increasing expectation for high performance. These factors can exhaust employees and lead to burnout if not managed well.

Secondly, there is a greater societal recognition of mental health as a crucial determinant of overall wellness—both in and out of the workplace.

5.2. Leadership Traits for Mental Well-being

Leadership strategies for fostering mental well-being in the workplace stem from specific leadership traits.

- Empathy: Active understanding and sharing of another person's emotions and experiences. Effective leaders empathize with their team members and create an environment that values emotional connection and understanding.

- Emotional Intelligence: The ability to perceive, regulate, and communicate emotions, and to understand emotions in others. Emotional intelligence enhances leaders' ability to navigate stressful situations and lead with sensitivity.

- Authenticity: Genuine leadership is grounded in truthful relations. An authentic leader is self-aware, transparent, ethical, and open-minded. These qualities foster trust and create a psychologically safe work environment, conducive to mental health.

- Resilience: Leadership resilience refers to the ability to bounce back from adversity, keep a positive perspective, and maintain focus in challenging circumstances. Resilient leaders cultivate resilient teams, shaping cultures that view setbacks as learning opportunities rather than failures.

5.3. Practical Strategies for Leaders

Leaders can shape mental wellness at work by integrating certain practices into their leadership approach.

1. Open Communication: Encourage team members to express their

feelings and concerns without fear of judgment or negative repercussions.

2. Flexible Work Arrangements: Offering flexibility such as remote work options or flexible hours can greatly reduce stress and contribute to better mental health.

3. Regular Check-ins: Checking in on employees' well-being demonstrates care and cultivates trust. This could be through weekly one-on-one meetings, group sessions, or casual conversations.

4. Resources and Training: Provide resources that educate about mental health and train supervisors to better support their teams. This could involve bringing in mental health professionals for workshops or providing resources for self-paced learning.

5. Recognition and Appreciation: Regularly recognizing and appreciating employees' efforts can boost their esteem and satisfaction, promoting mental wellness.

5.4. The Long-term Impact of Leadership-Driven Mental Wellness Initiatives

When leaders prioritize mental wellness, the effects ripple through the organization. This focus creates a psychologically safe environment, where individuals feel they can be their authentic selves without fear of stigma or reprisal.

This openness boosts employee engagement, satisfaction, and loyalty. It provides the support frameworks necessary for individuals to seek help if they're struggling, reducing the risk of burnout and increasing overall productivity.

Notably, when employees feel mentally healthy, they're likely to be more creative and innovative—a win-win situation that benefits both the individual and the organization.

To recap, the role of leadership in cultivating mental well-being is a potent one. But it is not an innate skill; it is achievable, requiring continuous learning and development. As leaders embody these strategies and cultivate mental wellness, they inspire better organizational performance, resilience, and innovation in the workplace. Moving forward, as we redefine leadership, mental wellness deserves a place at the heart of the conversation.

Chapter 6. Incorporating Mindfulness into Your Leadership Style

Mindfulness, often described as the capacity to be fully aware of the present moment, has been gaining traction in various fields, including leadership. It represents an essential quality for leaders who want to foster an environment of mental wellness, reducing stress levels and increasing their team's productivity. Herein lies the essence of mindful leadership.

6.1. The Pillars of Mindful Leadership

A mindful leader fosters a positive mindset and promotes mental wellbeing through a leadership style that embodies three core principles: awareness, presence, and intentionality.

Awareness of one's own actions, emotions, and thoughts is the first pillar of mindful leadership. Mindful leaders are constantly aware of their inner world and how it shapes their interactions with others. They recognize when their stress levels are escalating and use mindfulness techniques to manage these emotions.

Presence is the potent state of being 'in the now.' This means avoiding multi-tasking, refraining from thinking about past or future ventures when in a meeting or discussion, and giving coworkers and employees undivided attention. Mindful leaders value the power of presence to improve the clarity of communication, foster authenticity, and build trust.

Intentionality involves making deliberate, conscious decisions.

Mindful leaders are aware of why they are making certain decisions and take into account their potential impact on others. They also promote a culture of intentionality, by encouraging coworkers and employees to think through their choices and actions.

6.2. Developing Mindful Leadership Habits

As a leader, integrating mindfulness into your leadership style is a continuous process. There are several approaches that can help develop these mindful habits:

Daily Mindfulness Practice: Daily meditation or mindfulness exercises can enhance your ability to be fully present and reduce your stress levels. During times of high stress, these techniques can help you maintain your composure and make wise, thoughtful choices.

Mindful Communication: Mindful communication promotes clarity, reduces misunderstandings, and fosters an environment of mutual respect. One way to practice mindful communication is active listening, where you fully focus on the speaker and respond with empathy and respect.

Self-reflection: A critical but often overlooked aspect of leadership, reflection allows you to assess your actions and decisions. Regular self-reflection can help you recognize any gaps in your leadership style, identify areas for improvement, and assess your emotional well-being.

6.3. Promoting Mindfulness within the Team

Inspiring others towards mindfulness goes beyond modeling mindful behaviors; you need to actively promote mindfulness practices within your team. Here are a few ways to establish a culture of mindfulness:

Workshops and Training: Consider arranging mindfulness workshops and training sessions for your team. These can range from teaching simple mindfulness exercises to more in-depth courses on mindfulness-based stress reduction.

Creating a Mindful Environment: Cultivate a work environment that appreciates mindfulness. This could mean implementing designated quiet spaces for meditation or simply encouraging your team to take regular breaks to refresh and refocus.

Encouraging Openness and Vulnerability: Foster a culture that allows individuals to express their thoughts and feelings without fear of judgment. This openness can reduce stress, increase mutual respect, and foster a positive working environment.

6.4. Overcoming Challenges in Incorporating Mindfulness

The road to mindful leadership isn't without its hurdles. Common challenges include skepticism from team members, difficulty in maintaining consistency, and managing expectations.

It's important to stay patient, remain authentic, and continue practicing mindfulness, even in the face of resistance. Moreover, it's essential to remember that mindfulness is not a 'quick fix' solution, but rather a long-term commitment that requires patience, practice, and continual learning.

In conclusion, mindful leadership promises compelling benefits both for individual leaders and their teams. Not only does it provide effective tools to manage stress, but it also fosters a positive, efficient, creative, and mentally wellness-oriented workplace. Embrace the journey of developing your mindful leadership style — it will undoubtedly be a transformative and rewarding experience.

Chapter 7. Techniques to Promote Mental Wellness among Employees

The awareness about mental wellness is gradually seeping into the workplace, but its true potential is just beginning to be realized. Many organizations are introducing policies that acknowledge the importance of mental health, but there's more to be done. After all, mental wellness influences so much more than just the atmosphere in the office – it affects performance, productivity, and even overall business success. Here are some key techniques organizations and team leaders can implement to promote mental wellness among employees.

7.1. Breaking Stigma and Dispelling Myths

Mental wellness remains a stigma-ridden subject in many workplaces where employees often hesitate to discuss or disclose their mental health concerns for fear of prejudice or discrimination. Employers can effectively tackle this hurdle by promoting an open and supportive environment.

- Proactive communication: Use different forums, such as team meetings, seminars, and newsletters, to discuss mental health openly.

- Educate and enlighten: Run training sessions about common mental health conditions and their symptoms, encouraging the team to identify and accommodate colleagues struggling with mental health issues.

- Encourage self-care: Foster an environment which values self-care and work-life balance.

7.2. Training the Mind: Mindfulness and Meditation

Mindfulness and meditation exercises can significantly enhance cognitive abilities, helping employees engage more effectively in their tasks and manage workplace stressors.

- Mindfulness training programs: Conduct regular training programs that discuss the principles of mindfulness, teaching employees practical ways to introduce these principles into their work routines.

- Incorporating Meditation: Provide dedicated spaces and time slots to employees for practicing meditation during office hours.

7.3. The Power of Flexibility

A rigid workspace can be stressful and overwhelming. Offering a more flexible work environment can substantially improve overall mental well-being.

- Flexible work hours: Allow employees to set their working hours, within reason. This helps alleviate stress related to balancing the demands of work, personal life, and family.

- Remote work: Provide opportunities for remote work. Not only will this minimize work-related travel stress but also allows employees to work in a setting where they are most comfortable.

7.4. Fostering a Supportive Environment

Creating an environment that is supportive and non-judgmental can encourage employees to adopt a healthier mindset and feel more secure at work.

- Peer support: Encourage camaraderie among team members. This creates a feeling of community, offers emotional support, and assists employees in dealing with work-related pressures.

- Managerial support: Train managers to recognize the signs of mental health struggles and to offer supportive responses.

7.5. Implementing Wellness Programs

Incorporating wellness programs within your organization can foster an awareness and understanding of mental health, and provide skills and strategies to manage it.

- Holistic Wellness Programs: Implement programs that address more than just physical health. Offer tools and resources for stress management, mental health screenings, counseling services, and more.

- Continuous learning programs: Educate employees about mental health and self-care strategies on an ongoing basis.

7.6. Empowering through Autonomy

Giving employees the freedom to control their work can result in improved satisfaction, productivity and overall mental wellbeing.

- Encourage decision-making: Involve employees in the decision-making process. This involvement imparts a sense of control, increasing confidence, and reducing job stress.

- Task ownership: Allow employees to take ownership of their tasks, thereby creating a sense of responsibility and motivation.

7.7. Recognizing and Rewarding Efforts

Acknowledgement of effort helps assure employees that they are valued, contributing to increased confidence and motivation.

- Regular Recognition: Regularly recognizing employees for their achievements is a powerful mental wellness booster.

- Rewards: Offer tangible rewards, such as bonuses, time-off, or gifts, to further encourage positive behavior.

Achieving workplace mental wellness is a journey that requires consistent efforts and an open-minded approach. By integrating these practices into your company culture, you enable your employees to carve a path towards mental wellness. In turn, enabling your organization to revel in the myriad of benefits that a mentally healthy workplace provides. Remember that mental health is not a luxury – it's a critical aspect of overall health. And in the workplace, it can be your fastest route to exceptional growth and unparalleled success.

Chapter 8. Case Studies: Successful Mindful Leadership in Action

Undoubtedly, the best way to understand the impact of mindful leadership is to observe it in action. Evaluating the success stories of mindful leadership at different companies offers a coherent understanding of this approach and its positive effects on mental wellness in the workplace.

8.1. Google's "Search Inside Yourself" Program

Google, a company recognized for its forward-thinking environment, integrated mindfulness into its corporate culture with its ground-breaking "Search Inside Yourself" program. Initially launched by Chade-Meng Tan, a Google engineer, this initiative advocates for mindfulness and emotional intelligence in the workplace.

Tan's vision led to a two-day course for employees focusing on three key areas: mindfulness, self-awareness, and emotional intelligence. These elements were considered the building blocks for increasing productivity, fostering innovation, and promoting a positive work environment.

Studies suggest that Google employees reported feeling calmer, more patient, and better able to listen after participating in the course. They also reported a heightened ability to handle and recover from challenging situations, indicating that this mindfulness program indeed improved workplace cohesiveness and productivity. The success of the "Search Inside Yourself" program propels a compelling case for mindful leadership.

8.2. Aetna's Mindfulness and Yoga Programs

When Aetna CEO Mark Bertolini collided with a ski accident, resorting to yoga and mindfulness, he realized their remarkable impacts. He decided to introduce them to his employees, with the aim to reduce stress and improve responses to demanding work situations.

Aetna launched mindfulness practices and yoga programs amongst its employees and discovered a notable increase in productivity—roughly an extra hour each week per participating employee. Moreover, participants reported considerable improvements in their perceived stress levels.

After introducing mindfulness, Aetna saved about $2000 per employee in healthcare costs and gained $3000 per employee in productivity – a compelling illustration of the monetary advantages of fostering mental wellness.

8.3. The SAP Social Sabbatical Program

SAP, the software giant, has approached mindful leadership from a somewhat different angle. Their Social Sabbatical program allows employees to take a short break from their usual roles to work on socially impactful projects. This initiative helps employees expand their perspectives, mitigate burnout, and bolster individual resilience.

As per reports, the program had a profoundly positive effect on participating employees. They reported improved skills, heightened self-confidence, and a better understanding of new cultures and perspectives, contributing to greater innovation capacity and improved solutions to business problems.

8.4. Intel's Mindfulness Program

Intel introduced a mindfulness program titled "Awake@Intel", which incorporated regular quiet periods into the workday, mindfulness classes, and online resources. The program was voluntary, attracting those open to the concept of mental wellness.

The benefits were duly noted – there was a significant decrease in reported stress levels and an increase in overall happiness and feelings of engagement at work post this program's rollout. Similarly, Intel found a 13% increase in the perceived amount of time participants had to get things done—an indicator of enhanced productivity borne of mindful leadership.

8.5. Walmart's Supportive Leadership

Walmart, often criticized for their management approach, introduced a support-oriented leadership development strategy rooted in empathy and emotional intelligence. They provided hundreds of managers with extensive workshops emphasizing communication, employee wellbeing, and positive psychology.

The results showed that stores whose managers participated in the program outperformed those that did not, in critical areas like sales growth and customer satisfaction. Improved mental wellness amongst Walmart's managers significantly impacted the overall store performance.

These examples illuminate the positive real-world impacts of mindful leadership. For these organizations, integrating mindfulness resulted in ascendant productivity, reduced stress, improved focus, and increased employee satisfaction—a testament to the value of investing in mental wellness in the workplace.

Chapter 9. Strategies for Managing Workplace Stress

Recognizing the role that stress plays in workers' lives is a critical starting point for any leader aspiring to create a healthier working environment. Stress is woven into our everyday lives, and while some degree of pressure can propel us forward, excessive amounts can damage our health and impede our productivity.

9.1. Understanding Workplace Stress

Stress in the workplace can stem from a myriad of sources, ranging from high workload pressures to lack of role clarity, challenges in managing work-life balance, strained interpersonal relationships, and more. Understanding the conditions that generate stress is fundamental in determining the best strategies to manage it.

In a survey by the American Psychological Association in 2017, 61% of Americans listed work as a significant source of stress. A European Agency for Safety and Health at Work survey conducted in the same year revealed that 51% of workers found work-related stress to be common in their workplace.

Managing stress figures prominently in the responsibilities of a mindful leader. Ignoring the signals of stress can lead to chronic health conditions like depression, anxiety disorders, cardiovascular disease, and others, directly affecting the individuals concerned and potentially leading to increased absenteeism and decreased work performance.

9.2. Identifying Sources of Stress

Identifying stressors is key in creating effective strategies to address them. Common workplace stressors include lack of control over work, high demands, unclear job expectations, dysfunctional workplace dynamics, lack of social support, lack of work-life balance, and fear of job redundancy.

Creating a culture of open communication and incentivizing anonymous feedback can help leaders identify these stressors. The clarity of vision and execution that a leader provides can make sense of job roles and ease feelings of frustration or confusion. A supportive workplace culture that prizes camaraderie and inclusivity can also alleviate stress.

9.3. Building Personal Resilience

Resilience refers to an individual's capacity to withstand and bounce back from adversity. It determines one's ability to maintain mental wellness under high stress levels. While it's partly an inherent trait, it can be developed and strengthened with practice.

Mindfulness - paying attention on purpose, non-judgmentally, in the present moment - is a noteworthy practice in fostering resilience. A research study by Kabat-Zinn (2003) showed an increase in levels of resilience in employees who underwent an eight-week mindfulness training program.

Moreover, regular break times, work-life balance, regular physical activity, healthy diet, adequate sleep, fostering positive relationships, finding meaning in work, and seeking professional help when needed - all these contribute to personal resilience.

9.4. Implementing Stress Management Programs

Many companies are starting to recognize the economic and health benefits of implementing stress management programs. Organizational change to reduce work stress might include redesigning jobs to provide workers with more control, increasing recognition of employees' efforts and achievements, improving working conditions, or offering work flexibility solutions.

Offering programs such as yoga and meditation classes, resilience workshops, mental health days, and confidential counseling services can be beneficial. Employee Assistance Programs and mental health awareness programs are also commonly offered in many organizations.

9.5. Prioritizing a Balanced Work-Life Culture

It's paramount that leaders prioritize a balanced work-life culture. Employees who can balance their work and personal life are often more productive, happier, and less stressed. Flexible working hours, remote work opportunities, discouraging overtime, encouraging vacation time, and offering maternity and paternity leave – these are all strategies to promote a balanced work-life culture.

Leadership can play a significant role in directly promoting this balance, setting an example, and encouraging others to follow suit. It's crucial to have leaders who can demonstrate that it's possible to be successful in their roles without sacrificing personal health and happiness.

9.6. Cultivating a Supportive Work Environment

A supportive work environment can reduce workplace stress and foster mental wellness. Encouraging teamwork, promoting open communication, providing training and development opportunities, fostering trust, and recognizing achievements all contribute to a supportive work environment and higher job satisfaction.

Organizations can promote mental wellness by providing an inclusive and respectful workplace culture, taking a proactive stance towards mental health at work by investing in mental wellness programs, and maintaining a work environment that respects individual needs.

Ultimately, keeping up with the rapidly evolving workplace environment requires adaptability, openness, and a commitment to prioritize the mental wellness of your team. By implementing strategies to manage stress effectively, you can create a work environment where individuals thrive, and an organization that fosters creativity, innovation, and productivity.

As leaders, the choice is yours. Choose well-being, choose success. Your commitment to creating a mentally healthy workplace can serve as an example for your employees, boost morale, productivity, and workplace satisfaction, consequently fostering a uniquely positive company culture.

Chapter 10. Building Resilience and Fostering Innovation through Mindfulness

The recognition of the integral role that mental wellness plays in the workplace has become an increasing priority for leaders across industries. Building resilience and fostering innovation are two core components of promoting mental wellness, and mindfulness is a tool that can remarkably facilitate these processes.

Mindfulness itself, rather than being a buzzword or a transient trend, is a time-honoured practice rooted in ancient wisdom, which has found continuing relevance in today's frenzied work environment. The heart of mindfulness lies in harnessing and expanding the capability to live in the present moment, unswayed by the pulls of the past or the anxieties of the future.

10.1. The Interrelation of Resilience, Innovation, and Mindfulness

It's crucial to understand the intricate web that connects resilience, innovation, and mindfulness. Resilience in the workplace context refers to an individual's ability to bounce back from setbacks, adapt well to change, and keep going even in the face of adversity. Innovation, a much sought-after attribute, involves thinking out of the box, challenging the status quo, and coming up with fresh ideas and solutions. It is the driving force behind business growth and competitive advantage in the modern market.

Mindfulness serves as the underpinning that fosters both resilience and innovation. It encourages us to maintain an open mindset, ceaselessly learn and adapt, and persist with a positive outlook, even under immense stress or challenging circumstances. Through mindfulness, leaders can help their teams enhance resilience and stimulate innovative thinking by nurturing a mentally healthy environment.

10.2. Building Resilience through Mindfulness

Resilience is not a trait that people either have or don't have. It's a skill that's developed through lived experiences, and it can be honed and strengthened. By adopting mindfulness, individuals can remarkably cultivate their resilience.

Mindfulness aids in the development of resilience by promoting the understanding of emotion. When one is consistently mindful, it becomes easier to recognize, acknowledge, and accept challenging emotions rather than resisting or suppressing them. By recognizing the temporary nature of these emotions, one is encouraged to approach adversities with a problem-solving mindset, thereby strengthening their resilience.

Additionally, mindfulness facilitates resilience by promoting self-compassion. With consistent mindfulness practice, individuals learn to treat themselves with kindness and forgiveness, especially in moments of failure or difficulty. This self-compassion bolsters resilience levels, allowing individuals to recover more quickly from failures or setbacks.

Within an organizational context, leaders can nurture resilience by integrating mindfulness into the workplace culture. Initiatives like mindfulness workshops and trainings or creating quiet, mindful spaces within the office can help promote a resilient mindset in teams.

10.3. Inspiring Innovation through Mindfulness: A Paradigm Shift

Mindfulness can create a long-term, organization-wide shift in innovative thinking when leaders embed it as a key aspect of company culture. This shift is a result of the change mindfulness inspires on an individual level.

By focusing attention on the present moment, mindfulness encourages greater awareness of one's surroundings, often leading to fresh perspectives and ideas. It pushes individuals to explore new ways of thinking and challenges them to venture outside their comfort zones.

Moreover, mindful leaders inspire teams to detach from the fear of failure, thereby fostering a culture of creative exploration. As employees feel safe and supported in their attempt to innovate, the organization benefits from an influx of fresh, valuable ideas.

Organizations can encourage innovative thinking by making mindfulness a routine aspect of their work processes. Regular mindfulness training sessions are beneficial, as well as incorporating mindful practices into team meetings, such as a few minutes of collective silence or a conscious check-in at the start to help everyone be fully present.

10.4. Creating a Culture of Mindful Leadership

A culture of mindful leadership is key in transforming any organization into a supportive, innovative, and resilient workplace. Leaders employing mindfulness practice set an example for their teams, and they are instrumental in advancing mental wellness at work.

Mindful leaders display empathy, which helps in understanding team members' strengths, weaknesses, and unique perspectives. This understanding is crucial for assigning the right tasks to the right individuals and fostering an environment where everyone feels valued.

In addition, embracing mindfulness allows leaders to make well-considered decisions. By being fully present, leaders can attentively listen, understand, and assess various perspectives before making a decision. This way, the emotional intelligence of the leader is enhanced, contributing to better team morale, productivity, and ultimately, increased organizational success.

Every journey towards becoming a mindful leader starts with the self. Leaders can start by incorporating mindfulness in daily routines, like mindful breathing, walking, or eating. Following a regular meditation schedule or attending mindfulness retreats can also be beneficial in deepening the practice.

10.5. Conclusion

While a challenging task, incorporating mindfulness into workplace culture presents a promising pathway to developing resilience and fostering innovation. It's not a switch that leaders can simply flip; it requires continuous effort and deliberate strategy. However, the long-term benefits for individuals and organizations alike are significant. With practical mindfulness interventions and mindful leadership, a positive and growth-oriented workplace culture can be cultivated, linking mental wellness and business success in a thoroughly harmonious relationship.

Chapter 11. The Future of Work: A New Era of Mindful Leadership

As we stand on the cusp of a significant transformation in the world of work, it becomes essential to address the dynamics of evolving workplaces and their impact on leadership practices and mental wellness. As the boundaries of traditional office settings blur, it's time to decipher the underlining role of mindfulness and empathetic leadership shaping this new era.

11.1. The Shift Towards Remote Working

The COVID-19 pandemic has irreversibly altered the work landscape, pushing businesses worldwide to adopt remote working models. Even as the world inches towards health and normalcy, many companies, recognizing the benefits of these models, have continued them or adopted a hybrid approach. This shift has engendered new stressors among employees, relating to isolation, work-life integration, the lack of supervision, and even overworking. In response, leaders must cultivate a culture supporting mental health and adopt a mindful leadership approach to managing these transitions.

A mindful leader can drive fortitude in this new face of work by helping team members understand the importance of structured schedules, defining boundaries between their personal and professional lives, promoting flexibility, and emphasizing regular and effective communication. Longitudinal research on remote work has consistently shown that employee satisfaction, job performance, turnover intention, and work-related stress can drastically improve when leaders foster an atmosphere of trust, patience, and empathy.

11.2. Mindfulness in Leadership

The concept of mindfulness, originating from Buddhist traditions, has seen increasing acceptance in the corporate world in recent years. Mindfulness is the practice of focusing one's attention on the present moment in a non-judgmental way. Applied in the context of leadership, it includes being present, attentive, and non-judgmental in all interactions and decisions.

Enlightened by research findings, leading global companies are encouraging leaders to cultivate mindfulness skills. Programmes involving mindfulness training have shown to increase leaders' capacities for emotional regulation, empathy, flexible thinking, creativity, and decision-making.

These qualities empower leaders to manage team dynamics better, support employee well-being, and deliver superior results during times of uncertainty and change. They also help in avoiding the prevalent 'burnout culture,' where employees feel pressured to work relentlessly, leading to job dissatisfaction, attrition, and mental health concerns.

Moreover, mindfulness isn't just about personal introspection. When leaders exhibit mindfulness, they create a safe space for their teams to imitate the same behaviours, encouraging compassionate self-observation and promoting a healthier working environment.

11.3. Technological Influence on Mindful Leadership

AI and automation are increasingly undertaking repetitive tasks, freeing employees to engage more in intellectual, creative, and strategic pursuits. This paradigm shift necessitates that leaders focus not only on productivity and performance but also on nurturing creativity, problem solving, collaboration, and emotional intelligence within their teams.

Digital tools, like wearable devices and mental-health apps, are helping organizations track wellness metrics and offer personalized solutions for managing stress, anxiety, and other mental health issues. Leaders should endorse these resources and make mental health conversations mainstream to destigmatize them and encourage adoption.

11.4. Building a Mindful Corporate Culture

Embracing mental wellness in the workplace and building a mindful corporate culture asks for systemic changes. Leaders must demonstrate vulnerability and openness, acknowledging the presence of work-related stressors and their impact on mental health.

Leaders can also inspire mindfulness by aligning it with an organization's core values and integrating it into daily routines. It could include incorporating mindfulness training into employee development program, proposing 'no-meeting' blocks to allow focused work hours, or even dedicating quiet spaces in the office for reflection and relaxation.

11.5. The Way Forward

The future of work demands empathetic leaders, conscious of their actions, and their potential influence on their team's mental wellness. Embracing this new era of mindful leadership doesn't entail a complete overhaul but requires incremental changes like self-awareness, active listening, and compassionate interactions.

Remember, the journey of mindful leadership begins with oneself. It involves continual learning, reflection, and mindful execution, fostering an environment of trust, empathy, and holistic growth in the workplace. As we embrace this new era, the future of work indeed seems promising.

The power of mindful leadership and its impact on mental wellness in workplaces has a critical role in the successful businesses of the future. By prioritizing mental health and leading empathetically, organizations can uncover remarkable opportunities for growth, productivity, and positive culture shift as we head into a new, exciting era of work.

www.ingramcontent.com/pod-product-compliance
Lightning Source LLC
Chambersburg PA
CBHW062310290526
45794CB00006B/2745